From Award-Winning Entrepreneur

BUILD BEFORE 21

Don't wait to grow up, Grow by Building early.

By Tanweer Sidd

IMMERSION & BUILDER'S OATH

Your No-Excuses Guide to Building Early, Fast, and Smart

By Tanweer Sidd

Award-Winning Entrepreneur & Author

You're not just holding a book. You're holding a promise—a personal declaration that your journey won't be measured by years spent waiting, but by the things you choose to build before the world says you're ready.

Welcome to the Builder's Mindset

Run your fingers over the title—bold, audacious, almost defiant.
Build Before 21. The words aren't just designed for aesthetics; they're a challenge spelled out in the color of action, the shape of momentum, and the gravity of a milestone.

Imagine This...

It's late at night in Lucknow, ceiling fan humming, your phone screen glowing with yet another "success story" that feels impossibly distant. You wonder if the future you want is just for the privileged, the "well-connected," or those living in Silicon Valley.

But here's the truth:

Great things are started in small rooms, with more questions than answers, by those bold enough to begin.

Why This Book, Why Now?

I wrote this for you—the student staring down a syllabus and a blank screen, the dreamer who scrolls through job listings yet craves autonomy, the young creator who hasn't yet heard "yes" but refuses to be defeated by "not yet."

- If you've ever felt stuck, this book will show you movement.
- If you've wondered when it's your 'turn,' this will prove it's now.
- If you doubted whether starting small matters, you'll see it's the only way any real journey ever begins.

The Builder's Oath

"I promise not to wait until I'm 'old enough' or 'smart enough.

I will build before the world tells me I can.

My discipline matters more than my inheritance.

I am a builder—starting today."

Sign your name. Date this page. This is where your story begins.

The "Diguria Principle"

No matter where you are—city, small town, hostel room, or the corner booth of a late-night chai shop—momentum starts when you do. I began scribbling business models on exam answer sheets at Integral University, Lucknow. The size of your ambition is never determined by your starting place.

An Invitation

Before you turn the page, pause and answer honestly:

- What is one thing you want to build before your next birthday?
- Why now? Why not you?

Tear out this page, write your intention, and pin it up where you'll see it daily. Let this book be the blueprint you wish you had—detailed, actionable, and rooted in real, lived experience.

Because building before 21 isn't just a dare.

It's a decision. And your future starts here.

DEDICATION & RELATABLE OPENING

Dedication

For every young dreamer in a small town, a noisy household, a crowded metro, or a remote college hostel—

who's ever thought, "Am I too young? Too late? Too ordinary?"

For the builders who start with doubt in their pocket, not certainty.

For everyone who chose action over excuses, even when nobody was watching.

This book is for you.

A Very Familiar Beginning

When I began, I wasn't "the chosen one."
I worked from a shared room overlooking Lucknow's bustling streets, dodging neighbors' noise and watching power cuts throw my plans into darkness. Each evening, as the last light faded, I asked myself:

What if my ordinary is someone else's impossible starting point?
What if my limitations are really my launchpad?

I want you to know—I started confused. I started with free YouTube videos, dusty secondhand books, and the cheapest internet pack I could get. My first "team" was a group chat of friends who mostly ghosted me after the first week.
But each time I felt small, I wrote these lines on a scrap of paper taped above my study desk:

If you never look in the mirror of ambition, you'll always see the reflection of someone else's dreams."

I returned to that line every time I doubted myself. I hope you return to these pages every time you doubt yourself.

A Shared Promise

I don't know your hometown, your marksheet, or your family's story. But I know you have—right now—enough ambition, imagination, and stubbornness to create momentum that's real and lasting.
And that's all you truly need to start.

Let's dedicate every page after this to the first, imperfect, unstoppable steps you'll take.

[Turn the page. Your journey as a builder is already underway.]

EPIGRAPH & OPENING REFLECTION

Epigraph

"Start where you are. Use what you have. Do what you can."
— Arthur Ashe

The weight of these words shaped my earliest days as a builder. You don't need to be the richest student in the class, the best orator, or come from an influential family. You only need to begin with what's truly yours: your ideas, your time, and the willingness to act while others hesitate.

Why This Line Matters

I remember reading this quote in a dimly-lit library corner, with a power bank barely clinging to life and a mind flickering with doubts. At that moment, I realized that the world never gave permission slips to the people who built it; they gave themselves permission.

This is precisely why this epigraph stands alone here—because your journey, like every builder's, must begin with **where you are, what you have, and what you are ready to do now.**

Pause & Reflect

- Where are you right now—physically, emotionally, mentally?
- What do you have? (A notebook, a phone, an idea, a hunger to change?)
- What can you do this week, before reading page 10, to begin?

The smallest move is infinitely greater than the biggest intention that stays locked in your head.

Signature Prompt: Builder's Moment

Circle one:

- I'm ready to start, even if it's messy.
- I'm not sure how, but I'm open to becoming a builder.
- I've failed before, but I'll start again.

This is your story. This is your page.

[Turn the page: Let the building begin.]

COPYRIGHT, PUBLICATION DETAILS & BUILDER'S WELCOME

ISBN: **978-93-343-6033-2**

First Edition

Design & Layout: **Team - Tanweer Sidd**

"Self-published"

Contact: Books@Tanweersidd.com

Published in India. Any resemblance to real persons, events, or startup journeys is, in most cases, intentional.

🛠 Builder's Welcomelf

If you're reading this notice it means you respect the work, sweat, and sleepless nights poured into these pages—not only by me, but by every past builder who dared to dream out loud. Copyright isn't just legalese: it's a digital age reminder that your ideas, your momentum, and your story matter. Guard it, share what inspires, but always build your own path.

Think of this copyright page as your first lesson in ownership—not just of intellectual property, but of your own future.

You're not just a reader now. You're a builder.

And the world makes room for those who start.

[*Turn the page. The blueprint gets bolder from here.*]

Table of Contents

Part IV: Growth & Resilience

Part V: Multiply & Sustain

Resources & Appendices

[Turn the page. Let's begin the real work—your introduction awaits.]

When I first met Tanweer Sidd, he was not the loudest voice in the room—but he was always the one asking the most interesting questions. As a mentor, I have seen many students dream big, but rare is the young founder who moves from idea to action with as much discipline, tenacity, and humility as Tanweer.

In writing Build Before 21, Tanweer isn't just sharing a script of "success." He's offering a lived-in blueprint—a series of late nights, early mornings, small victories, painful mistakes, and hard-won lessons. What makes this book memorable is not just the advice, but the empathy behind every page. Tanweer knows what it feels like to be dismissed for your age, to build with zero connections, and to feel like an underdog in a noisy, competitive world.

But here is what also sets Tanweer apart:
He didn't wait for credentials, permission, or even a "perfect" plan. He started with what he had—a simple laptop, patchy Wi-Fi, a crowded Lucknow hostel, and a hunger to build. His journey from those modest beginnings to becoming an award-winning entrepreneur and mentor for thousands of students is proof of what is possible when courage meets consistency.

If you are a student, an aspiring creator, or someone tired of watching others win from the sidelines, this book is your permission slip. Every chapter offers not just knowledge, but a challenge—an invitation to stop waiting and start building now. Years from now, you may outgrow the desk or the city in which you start reading this, but the habits, grit, and vision you cultivate here will keep serving you for decades.

As you turn these pages, ask yourself:
What can I build before the world thinks I'm "ready"?
What legacy can I launch before 21, or 25, or 30?
There is no limit except that which you accept for yourself.

Build small, build smart, but above all—build.
The world needs more young builders. Let this be your blueprint.

Ready for page 16?

Preface / Author's Note

My Invitation to "Builders"

Welcome to Build Before 21. You might be a student chasing grades, a hustler testing ideas after midnight, or someone who feels like the only builder in the room full of drifters. No matter your label, your city, or your circumstances—this book is for you.

Why I Wrote This

The most honest answer?

Because I was tired of waiting for "the right time."

At 16, I sat by a wobbly desk in Lucknow, laptop lid battered and aspirations bigger than my resources. Every voice—sometimes even my own—asked: "Who are you to build something new?"

I didn't fit the founder profile. No family money. No English boarding school. No "network."

But I had ambition that kept me restless, and a question I couldn't shake: Why not me? Why not now?

What You'll Find Here

- Transparent stories: The moments when things failed spectacularly and when small wins changed everything.
- Field-tested blueprints: Action sheets, self-audits, and challenges I used (and still use) to keep momentum real.

- **No theory without proof**: Each lesson is backed by what worked in my college hostel, during power cuts, or from pitching ideas with trembling hands

How to Use This Book

- Don't just read—act on it. Tackle the challenges at the end of every chapter.
- Reflect in the blank spaces. This book is meant to be underlined, scribbled in, personalized.
- Share your journey. Email, DM, or tag me when you build something—let's create a community of action-takers.

One Last Promise

You don't have to have all the answers to start.

You just have to move.

Momentum makes the world notice even the quietest whisper.

Are you ready to become a builder?

Let's start, together.

— **Tanweer Sidd**

Part - I
The Mindset Shift

Introduction – Your Wake-Up Call

Why This Isn't Just Another Book

If you picked up Build Before 21, chances are you're hungry for something real.
Not empty motivation. Not recycled advice. Not dreams that fizzle out the moment your phone buzzes.

You're here because a part of you refuses to wait for a sign or "permission." Maybe your journey began as mine did: in late-night solitude, eyes stinging from another digital rabbit hole—stories of founders and doers lighting up the screen. I wasn't chosen by any secret club. No trust fund. No famous last name. I started in a single room, in a city most maps ignore, with only my doubts for company and a stubborn itch to build.

The Cost of Inaction

Here's what I learned early and hard:
"The only real failure in your twenties is inaction. The rest is trial and error."
(Tony Fadell, inventor of the iPod & iPhone, echoes this truth: the world is built by those who stumble, learn, and keep moving. Sitting still only guarantees you miss out.)
For most of us, the myth is that you need perfect timing, a grand plan, or a world-shifting idea. The reality? Even the best ideas will

wither without action. I watched classmates wait for graduation, wait for the "right" job, wait for more certainty—and I watched their momentum, and confidence, shrink with each passing semester.

when you act—however awkwardly, imperfectly—you build experience. Experience compounds. Each small step sets you apart from the masses still waiting for guarantees.

Why "Build Before 21"?

- **21** isn't just an age.
- It's a symbol of the crossroads—when the pressure to follow the crowd or settle down becomes overwhelming. It's young enough to mess up, pivot, and start over, yet old enough to take ownership of your vision.
- Research shows early actors—those who start projects, businesses, creative work in their teens or early 20s—are more adaptive, resilient, and likely to find purpose that sticks (see James Clear's "atomic habits," which prove that small, early efforts lead to massive change over time)5.

- The only thing separating creators from dreamers is the courage to start before certainty arrives.

A Moment of Truth: My Starting Line

Let's be honest: My own "Page 1" wasn't impressive.

I failed at my first website launch. My early pitches went ignored. I sent cold emails from borrowed smartphones on patchy internet, with no backup plan if things collapsed. Each embarrassing start-up, every "no-response", " felt like a crack in the dream—until I realized each crack let knowledge and clarity seep in.

Every action, no matter how scrappy, is a brick in your foundation

Signature Prompt: Your Builder's Alarm

***Find a quiet corner. Write down:**

1. What's one thing you've put off out of fear, perfectionism, or waiting for "the right time"?
2. What's the smallest next step you can take today—even if you're not sure it will work?*

Print it. Tape it up. Read it every time you're tempted to hit pause on your progress.

You've just woken up to your real journey—the one that refuses to rewind or conform. The rest of this book is your blueprint for bold, imperfect, relentless building. Are you ready?

[Turn the page, and let action be your new habit.]

CLARITY OVER CONFUSION – WHY MOST WAIT

The Invisible Barrier

Every young builder faces an invisible force stronger than lack of money or connections: **confusion.**

You don't start building because someone said "wait until you're ready," or because every adult in your life asks, "What's your plan?" when you haven't even figured out what makes you feel alive.

I remember staring at my ceiling at 2 a.m., the fan spinning just above my doubts. College deadlines loomed. Notifications reminded me of all the things everyone else was doing.

My mind raced with questions:

- Is this even the right idea?
- What if I fail and people notice?
- Should I wait until I finish my degree—am I rushing things?

Then I realized: **The world is full of people waiting.**

Waiting for a job offer, waiting for their big break, waiting to "grow up." But behind every person you admire—every entrepreneur, artist, writer—there is always a quiet rebellion against waiting.

What Science Says About Starting

Neuroscience research shows when we delay action, our brains trigger anxiety and self-doubt loops. The longer we stall, the harder it is to begin.

According to Dr. Tim Pychyl, author of Solving the Procrastination Puzzle, "Action isn't just the effect of motivation, but also the cause of it."You build clarity by doing, not by sitting still.

Breaking the Myth: "You Need to Be Ready"

Readiness is a myth cooked up by fear and tradition.

- No startup founder I've met (including me!) ever felt ready to send the first pitch or build that first product.
- The only difference between those who build early and those who don't is the ability to act while confused, to learn by doing—not by waiting for perfect understanding.

Personal Story: Paralyzed by Planning

When I first imagined Sidd Infotech, I spent weeks sketching logos, dreaming of launch parties, and writing page after page of to-do lists—without ever actually starting. I was afraid my first step would be the wrong one, so I rehearsed instead of building.

It was only after sending one imperfect, typo-filled email to a possible client that momentum unlocked. The to-do lists didn't matter—movement did.

The Signature Shift

Builders gain clarity by building, not by thinking.

Want to kill confusion? Take a single, tangible step—even if it's halfway in the dark.

Your Turn — Action Worksheet

Grab a notebook.Write these three things:

- The one area you feel most confused about right now.
- The smallest step you could take before sleep tonight (DM a mentor, draft a project name, watch a 10-minute tutorial).

- The feeling you expect to have after acting (Relief? Excitement?Even more questions?).

You don't need a map to exit confusion. You need momentum—one brick at a time.

Clarity isn't magic. It's a byproduct of action. The only question is:

Will you be the one who keeps waiting, or the one who starts building —today

[Turn the page. Your first action awaits.]

Unlocking Your "Why" & Non-Negotiables

Why "Why" Matters

Beneath every big leap, every early morning, every restart after rejection—there's a reason deeper than "money" or "fame."

If you don't know your "why," you'll drift with every new trend, every voice that's louder than yours. The builders who last are those who have anchored their work in something unshakeable.

It took me months to pin down mine. I originally thought my "why" was to prove doubters wrong or earn more than a typical degree would promise. But those were shallow. The real fire was about building something meaningful, proving to myself that ordinary extraordinary by could become extraordinary by stubborn effort.

.

Discovering Your "Why": The 5-Whys Exercise

- Why do you want to build before 21?

(Your first answer: "To be independent.")

- Why is independence important to you?

("So I can make choices without fear.")

- Why do you fear losing freedom?

("Because I watched others feel trapped in jobs they hate.")

- Why do you want a different path?

("Because I believe I'm meant to create, not conform.")

- Why does this matter to you above all?

("Because I want to wake up proud of how I spent my twenties.")

Keep drilling down. The answer that "hurts a little" or scares you? That's usually the truth.

Setting Your Non-Negotiables

If your "why" is your compass, your non-negotiables are the boundaries that keep you on track.

What are non-negotiables?

They're your lines in the sand—the values, habits, or standards you refuse to compromise. They defend you from shiny objects, burnout, and chasing approval

Examples from My Journey

- **Never take on a project I wouldn't be proud to explain to my younger siblings.**
- **No skipping health for hustle:** A daily walk, home-cooked food, deep rest every week.
- **Protect time for learning:** 20 minutes a day—no matter what else is on the calendar.
- **Never use shortcuts that hurt my integrity:** Even if money or recognition dangles on the other side.

Your list will be different. What matters is the honesty and discipline behind it.

Builder's Worksheet

Take a page from your notebook and:

1. Write your "why" in one sentence, even if it feels raw or unfinished.

2.List three things you will not compromise on—even for a tempting shortcut or fast success.

3. Place this list somewhere visible (mirror, desk, phone lock screen).

Signature Prompt:

Tomorrow, when a hard decision comes, read your "why."

Remind yourself: Builders with purpose outlast everyone else.

Real Story: My "Why" in the Trenches

There was a night when an investor offered fast cash—but asked me to fudge user numbers. My "why" kept me from saying yes. I walked away, scared but proud. Months later, I signed my first real client, on my own terms. No "why," no line. No "line," no legacy.

Clarity fuels action. *"Why" gives courage. Turn the page to shape the mindset that takes you from consumer to creator.*

Mindset Shifts – From Consumer to Creator

Why Most People Stay Consumers

The world is engineered to turn you into a consumer. Notifications ping. Ads promise easy wins. Scrolling demands nothing but your time. Most people will spend years sharing, liking, reacting—but almost never creating. You might know someone who talks about starting a podcast, app, or business every week, but never ships a single thing.

My Turning Point

My story wasn't different. During my first semester at Integral University, my phone became my escape. I could quote YouTubers, knew which founders were trending, but had nothing to show for it except a meticulously curated playlist of other people's progress.

One night, I looked back on my month: hours lost scrolling, zero new skills practiced, nothing built. The realization stung.

The Three Laws of Creator Mindset

1.Production Beats Perfection:

You will never feel "ready." The act of putting something out—no matter how rough—trains your brain to see yourself as a builder, not just a watcher.

2.Progress Loves Consistency:

One post, one tweak, one attempt daily will always outweigh massive "someday" projects. Consistent creation stacks up skill, confidence, and audience.

3.Share as You Go:

When you build in public, you attract feedback, invite collaboration, and inspire the version of yourself that only exists in motion.

Action Exercise: The Consumption Audit

Take a page from your notebook:

- Track your digital activity tomorrow.
- Make three columns:
    a. Consuming (scrolling, watching, reading)
    b. Creating (writing, designing, coding, filming)
    c. Connecting (messaging, groups, comments with real purpose)
- At the end of the day, total up your hours.
- For one week, aim to add 15 minutes to your "creating" column each day—even if it's rough drafts, messy sketches, or voice notes nobody hears but you.

Signature Prompt: The "First Build" Challenge

- What is one simple thing you can create and share online—today?
- (A blog post, 30 seconds of advice, a basic website, a Canva graphic, an audio diary.)
- Post it.
- Share how it felt in your phone notes or journal.

Real Story: My First Video, My First Build

My first YouTube video was filmed in bad lighting, with my brother laughing in the background. There were three views (two were mine, one was my mom). But I hit Publish. That tiny act flipped a switch. In the weeks that followed, I wrote posts, coded a rough site, built a product that flopped. But I learned to love the process, not just the outcome. That's when real momentum began.

Takeaway: The Creator Identity Shift

You are not measured by what you consume, but by what you make, share, and test in the real world. Every small act of creation is a vote for your future builder identity.

From today, see the world as raw material.
Take one thing you learned, and turn it into something you build.
The next page begins your real, public journey as a creator.

Part - II
Set the Foundation

AUDITING YOUR CURRENT LIFE

Why Audit?

Most people drift—not because they lack ambition, but because they have no clear view of how their days are really spent. Before you build your future, you must map your present. This audit isn't about guilt; it's about awareness. You can only improve what you measure.

My First Reality Check

I remember the week I finally tracked my habits. I thought I was "busy" building. But when I actually wrote down my hours, the truth emerged:

- **12 hours** scrolling social feeds
- **8 hours** "researching" (just reading stories, not acting)
- **3 hours** real creation

My momentum wasn't stuck—I just hadn't seen the real scoreboard.

The Personal Audit Framework

Step 1: Track One Week.

- Use your phone, notebook or a Google Sheet.
- Divide each day into blocks: Morning, Afternoon, Evening, Late Night.

Step 2: Assign Categories.

- Consuming: (YouTube, Netflix, random browsing)
- Creating: (Coding, writing, recording, designing)
- Connecting: (Active social engagement with mentors ,builder or collaborators)
- Other: (Assignments, daily chores, rest)

Step 3: Be Ruthlessly Honest.

Yes, include "doing nothing" and "overthinking"—they count.

Step 4: Add Up Your Totals.

How much time is really invested in building, and how much is leaking away?

Day	Consuming	Creating	Connecting	Other
Monday	___	___	___	___
...	...	...	...	...
Total	___	___	___	___

Action Sheet: Your Personal Audit

- Print or draw the table above for the next 7 days.
- At the end of the week, circle the biggest "time leak."
- Reflect: What can I cut or replace to free up 30 minutes per day for creation?

Signature Prompt: The Builder's Mirror

"Momentum doesn't begin with ambition. It begins with radical honesty."

Look at your table. It isn't a judgment—it's your starting line.

Every great builder once faced a week that looked way messier than they hoped.

Real Builder Example: My Hidden Hours

when I uncovered the truth, I replaced just 30 minutes of scrolling with 30 minutes of writing daily. In three months, my first digital product was ready. One small shift can multiply your results more than you imagine.

Your audit isn't about perfection—it's the map that shows you which roads need new directions. Start tracking tonight. Tomorrow, your scoreboard changes.

[*Turn the page: Let's master time and energy for unstoppable building.*]

TIME MASTERY & ENERGY MANAGEMENT

The Time Illusion

Most of us feel like we never have enough time. University, side hustles, family responsibilities—your planner looks like a battleground, crammed with good intentions. But here's what I discovered:Time isn't the limiting factor—energy, intention, and focus are.

When I started building, I blamed time for slow progress. It was only when I learned to manage my energy and set real priorities that my projects moved forward.

The Cost of "Busy"

"Busy" is a badge people wear to avoid uncomfortable truths. My low-energy days would start with a snoozed alarm, drift into scattered multitasking, and end with regret—feeling "drained" but achieving very little.

What separates builders from drifters? Builders protect (and invest) their best hours where it matters most.

The "Prime Hour" Principle

Every builder has a window when they're sharpest—maybe you feel invincible at dawn, or supercharged after a late-night walk. This isn't about working more; it's about working smart:

- Find your Prime Hour: Track when you feel most focused during the week.
- Guard it ruthlessly: That's when you tackle real creation—writing, coding, pitching, or learning. Phone off, notifications silenced, no side tasks.

Action Sheet: Mapping Your Prime Hours

Track your energy for one week:

Day	Morning (1-10)	Afternoon (1-10)	Evening (1-10)	Notes
Monday				
...				
Sunday				

Reflect:

- Which blocks scored the highest?
- Where did you get the most deep work done?

Power Habits for Young Builders

- Start with ONE key task: Don't make a monster to-do list. Pick the most impactful task for your day and win that before anything else.
- Time blocking: Use a digital calendar or sticky notes to set "focus sprints" of 25-60 minutes.
- Protect your recharge: Sleep, nutrition, and breaks are assets, not luxuries. My best ideas arrived after a walk or a nap—not another hour online.

Signature Prompt: The "No-Zone" Ritual

- Choose one daily No-Zone: a phone-free, distraction-free block for real work—even just 30 minutes.
- Announce it to your family/team.
- At the end of each week, write what you built or learned during your "No-Zone.

Builder's Story: The Day I Stopped Multitasking

A week before my first major launch, I was frantically juggling customer calls, website edits, and social media—all at once. The result? Errors, exhaustion, and a product delay. Everything changed when I used my highest energy block exclusively for building. The quality skyrocketed, stress dropped, and my sense of momentum returned.

Takeaway : Time is Currency. Energy Is the Multiplier.

Every builder has 24 hours. The ones who win are those who invest attention where it changes the game.

Tonight, choose your Prime Hour for tomorrow. *T*urn the page ready to build, not just be busy.

IDENTIFYING HIGH-IMPACT SKILLS

Why Skills Matter More Than Credentials

In the digital world, what you can do opens more doors than where you studied or what grades you earned. Skills aren't just lines on your resume—they are the keys that give you actual leverage. Employers, partners, and customers look for proof you can execute, not just that you've attended classes.

Early in my journey, I realized that investing time into the right skills multiplied every opportunity. I built my first website with basic HTML learned from free online tutorials, closed my first client thanks to negotiation techniques from a INR 5 course, and later marketed my products using digital skills most students ignored. These weren't flashes of genius—just high-impact skills stacked, step by step.

Four Types of High-Impact Skills for Young Builders

1. **Digital Creation Skills**
    - Web development, graphic design, video editing, app building
    - Each lets you turn raw ideas into something others can see and use.
2. **Communication Skills**
    - Writing, public speaking, pitching, copywriting, storytelling
    - These unlock influence: the power to move people, share ideas, and get buy-in.

1. Modern Business Skills
    - Digital marketing, analytics, sales, customer service, negotiating deals
    - These are the backbone of every side hustle and scale-up project.
2. Self-Leadership Skills
    - Time management, goal setting, self-learning, stress management
    - They keep your momentum strong through chaos, rejection, and distractions.

Action Sheet: The Skill Scan

Step 1: List all skills you've touched in the past year.

(Include everything: coding, Canva, WhatsApp marketing, event hosting, tutoring, teamwork, etc.)

Step 2: In the following table, rate yourself "Starter," "Practicing," or "Confident" for each area.

Skill	Starter	Practicing	Confident
Example: Canva Design	✔		
Example: Negotiation		✔	
Example: Coding (HTML)			✔

Step 3: Circle one skill from each of the four categories above to focus on for the next 30 days.

Step 4: Find one free/affordable resource for each and set a daily practice commitment (15–30 minutes is enough)

Signature Prompt: The "Four-Stack Focus"

"Most people dabble, dabble, dabble. Builders stack, stack, stack—one high-impact skill at a time."

Write in your notebook:

- Which four skills will be your "Four-Stack" this month?
- What small daily action will move you from beginner to builder in each?

Builder Story: The Skill That Changed My Path

I didn't land my first big freelance client because of a degree—I was chosen because of a simple pitch deck I made in Canva. That client's feedback was, "I just need someone who gets digital branding and replies on time." Mastery in one practical skill rippled out to bigger wins, new clients, and eventually, my first full-time hire.

Your Next Move

Your skills—not your scorecard—are your superpower. Audit where you stand, set your 30-day focus, and stack your skills intentionally.

The next page unlocks how to leverage free resources and learning platforms so you don't need thousands to build your toolbox. Your stack starts here.

THE DIGITAL GOLDMINE MAP

Top Free Learning Platforms

- YouTube: For almost every skill (coding, design, business, speaking), there's a deep rabbit hole of genuinely high-quality, step-by-step tutorials. Filter by most recent for up-to-date guides.
- Coursera/edX: World-class universities offer free versions of many courses. Pay only if you want a certificate.
- Khan Academy: Perfect for revisiting the foundations—maths, basic finance, storytelling, and more.
- LinkedIn Learning: Sometimes free through your college or library, with bite-sized courses on personal branding, analytics, and tech.
- Skillshare: Free trials + occasional scholarships for creators serious about learning a new craft.

Special Mentions for Young Founders

- Google Digital Garage: Free modules on analytics, career skills, digital marketing—certified by Google.
- HubSpot Academy: Free digital marketing, sales, and growth hacking certificates. Perfect for side hustlers and early-stage founders.
- GitHub & Codepen: For developers, priceless for sharing and experimenting without cost.

Action Sheet: Your Learning Sprint

- Identify your top three skill gaps (from your Four-Stack on the last page.

- List at least two free platforms or resource links for each gap (Google search: "free [skill] course", e.g., "free negotiation course").
- Set a 21-day challenge: Commit to at least 20 minutes each day on focused, structured learning using these resources.

Skill to Build	Platform 1	Platform 2	Notes/Progress
Example: Canva	YouTube (Free)	Skillshare	Finished 30-min intro video
Example: Copywriting	HubSpot Academy	Coursera	Joined free course

Signature Prompt: Build Your Resource Rolodex

"You're never truly stuck if you're willing to learn for free and apply in public."

Start a digital doc or notebook—every time you find a resource, add it. Over a year, you'll have a powerful "growth stack" worth more than most paid degrees.

Builder Story: The Course That Cost Nothing—but Changed Everything

When I launched my first digital product, I knew nothing about sales funnels. Instead of hiring a consultant, I binge-watched a playlist on YouTube over one weekend, took notes, and applied just ONE idea. That tweak increased my conversions by 18% in a week. Best ROI I've ever had—zero money, all action.

Takeaway: Your Learning is Leverage

You don't need permission—or a limitless bank account—to start building mastery. Use this week to hunt, test, and immerse yourself in free learning. Let every new resource become a stepping stone to the next thing you build.

On the next page: You'll discover how to run experiments and ship real projects, no matter how small. Your foundation is set—now it's time for action.

PART - III
TAKE ACTION

SMALL EXPERIMENTS, FAST LAUNCHES

Why Experiments Beat Endless Planning

The myth of "the perfect plan" holds more builders back than lack of talent or funding. Every big success I've had started as a small, scrappy experiment: a mini-offer posted on social, a barebones landing page, a DM to a few potential users. When you treat ideas as prototypes—not masterpieces—momentum becomes your greatest ally.

The sooner you launch something real (however tiny), the faster you get feedback, learn what matters, and spot hidden opportunities.

My First Experiment: The 1,000-Rupee Test

Before Sidd Infotech ever saw a formal contract or website, I launched a test service: "Brand logo in 24 hours—₹1,000 flat." Posted it in three WhatsApp groups, DM'd connections, and waited. Was it glamorous? No. But within hours, I got my first paying client who became a long-term partner. That little test taught me more than months of "planning" could have.

The Micro-Launch Playbook

1. Pick an idea—strip it down to a core offer.
    - Can you explain it in a single sentence?
    - Is there ONE clear outcome for the customer or user?

2. Set a tiny test window.
    - 7 days, 10 customers, 1 week of daily stories—keep the scope small.
3. Launch before you're ready.
    - Share in group chats, social feeds, campus notices, or builder forums.
    - Don't aim for viral—aim for real usage or honest reactions.
4. Collect real feedback.
    - Three honest reviews matter more than 100 likes.
5. Iterate or kill fast.
    - "Boring" validation is great; silence tells you where to improve.

Idea	Simple Offer	Where to Launch	Timeline	Feedback?
Example: Logo Service	Logo/₹1,000 in 24h	WhatsApp groups	7 days	Yes (>1 client)
Example: Study Notes PDF	Downloadable eBook/₹49	Instagram Stories	3 days	5 DMs/questions

- Write yours below and commit to launching it within 3 days.

Signaure Prompt: The "Go Public" Challenge

"Don't spend three months polishing. Spend three hours launching. The world rewards action, not just intention."

Share your experiment—even if it flops. Every failed micro-launch brings you 10x closer to a breakout win (and gives you a story to tell that planners rarely have).

Builder Story: When My First Product Failed Forward

My first digital mini-course had zero signups on day one. I wanted to quit. But I asked every person who said "not interested" why. Their answers reshaped my content, price, and pitch. Three versions later, I broke even and found my first loyal subscribers. Fast launches = fast data = fast growth

Key Takeaway: Launch Before Perfect

No more waiting for "all green lights." Test wildly, launch cheap, improve publicly—and let your next experiment shape your first real win.

Up next: You'll discover how to turn small launches into a creator's habit—**the foundation for long-term success. Your next experiment starts now**.

THE MVP MINDSET – BUILD, SHIP, LEARN

Why "Minimum Viable Product" Wins

The world's best products didn't start as perfect—they launched as Minimum Viable Products (MVPs): the simplest version that solves one problem for real users. This concept changed my journey overnight. I used to obsess over features and polishing, worrying if my project looked "professional enough." Meanwhile, others were already learning, iterating, and improving out in the real world.
Building an MVP is about speed, feedback, and learning, not about looking flawless from day one.

The Real Value of Shipping Early

You don't truly know what works until you put it in front of someone else.
Your "almost ready" draft or hidden side project has zero impact until it's shipped—even if it isn't perfect.
Every launch is a combination of nerves, excitement, and the urge to cancel at the last minute. But every launch, good or bad, turns abstract ambition into real knowledge

The MVP Approach: Three Simple Steps

1. **Solve One Real Problem:**

Focus on the smallest, most painful challenge your user faces. Don't add features. Don't try to impress everyone.

2.**Build the Smallest Solution**

Can you deliver it in one week? If not, cut it in half.

- One-page website?
- Single tutorial video?
- Google Form or WhatsApp-based service?

3.**Get Real Feedback, Fast:**

Share with 3–5 honest people—friends, classmates, potential customers. Ask:

- Did it solve your problem?
- What confused or frustrated you?
- Would you pay or recommend it?

My MVP Journey: AffiliateKaro Beta

The first version of AffiliateKaro was literally a spreadsheet, a WhatsApp group, and a PDF guide. I was embarrassed, but people used it, pointed out flaws, and even requested features I never anticipated. By Month Two, what began as MVP was evolving, driven by actual user stories—not assumptions in my head.

Project / Idea	Core Problem	Simplest Version	Test Group	Feedback Questions
Example: Study Hub	Disorganized notes	WhatsApp group for doc sharing	4 classmates	Easy to use? What's missing? Join again?

- Fill in your own MVP idea in the table.
- Pick one idea to launch within 7 days.

Signature Prompt: MVP Promise

"I'd rather have a rough draft in the world than the perfect plan in my head."

Write down:

- Your one biggest excuse for not launching yet.
- The first step you'll take to turn your idea into an MVP this week.

Builder's Story: The Day "Perfect" Became My Biggest Enemy

During my first app build, I kept editing, redesigning, and second-guessing for months—until my mentor challenged me to launch as is and gather feedback. That version had bugs, but also enough real users to prove the idea was worth saving. Each release after that was 10x better because real feedback, not my inner critic, became my fuel.

Takeaway: Ship → Learn → Iterate

Your breakthrough won't come from a perfect start—but from real action, honest feedback, and relentless iteration.

The fastest way to learn is to launch, not to wait. Your MVP journey starts now.

FIRST MONETIZATION – SIDE HUSTLES & ONLINE INCOME

Why Earning Early Matters

It's easy to think, "Money will come once I have a big startup or get a 'real' job." But the fastest way to confidence—and freedom—is to make your first rupee, dollar, or sale before anyone expects you to. Your first side hustle (however tiny) teaches you more about markets, value, and resilience than any classroom ever will.

When my initial savings couldn't even buy a semester's worth of chai, I set a challenge: earn my first ₹500 online. Not as a favor, not from parents, but from delivering value to a stranger. That single act rewired my belief in what was possible.

The "Mini-Side Hustle" Game Plan

1. **Inventory Your Skills and Resources:**
    - What can you do better than a beginner? (Writing, Canva graphics, editing, social media, tutoring, coding, organizing events)
    - What access do you have? (Your college network, local WhatsApp groups, a unique perspective, a language skill)
2. **Pick a Micro-Offer:**

- **Product :** Sell notes, templates, digital art, pre-loved books.
- **Service:** Set up resumes, review applications, beta read, design profiles, weekly tutoring/coding help.

- **Platform:** Upwork, Fiverr, Facebook and WhatsApp groups, Notion, Gumroad, campus bulletins.

3.Set a Low Bar for Action:

- Launch with one offer to 10 people in your circle.
- Make it "impossible to refuse"—low-priced, high-value, specific promise ("I'll design your LinkedIn banner for ₹200," "Quick 30-min editing for your assignment").
- Don't over-engineer—sell, deliver, collect testimonials.

My First Online Income Story

I launched a handwritten revision notes PDF for classmates on WhatsApp: ₹49. In three days, 17 downloads. Did it change my life? No. But for the first time, money moved because of something I made. That spark created a feedback loop: confidence → skills → better offers → bigger pay.

Action Sheet: Your Side Hustle Challenge

Step 1: List three skills or things you can offer now.

Skill/Offer	Audience	Where to Sell/Post	Price	Time Frame
Example: Canva Designs	Classmates	WhatsApp Status/Story	₹200	1 week
Example: Resume Review	Seniors	LinkedIn/College forum	₹500	Next 10 days

Step 2: Pick the easiest one. Craft your offer in one line. Post it in two places/groups today.

Step 3: Mark when you get your first inquiry, client, or sale. Celebrate that momentum

Signature Prompt: Celebrate Small Wins

["You don't need a viral product to start winning. Your first ₹500 is your first brick—stack it, repeat, and watch belief multiply."]
Reward yourself for the first sale. Screenshot the message. Frame the note. Tell a friend. Build the habit of marking early progress.

Real Builder Insight: Money Follows Value

One DM, one gig, a single review—soon, word of mouth (and your skill) will do what ads cannot.
Takeaway: Start Now—No Excuses
Whether you're in a hostel, a remote village, or a metro city, there's someone who needs what you can do, today. Don't wait for "worthy"—act. Put up your offer. Ship your first product. Each side hustle is a classroom, and every rupee earned chips away at your old limits.

Next page: Turn your scattered wins into a habit by mastering routines and consistency—the true difference-maker between hobbyists and real builders.

THE POWER OF HABITS, ROUTINES, & CONSISTENCY

Why Habits Override Motivation

Ask any builder, athlete, or creator at the top of their field, and they'll admit: passion gets you started, but habits keep you building long after the initial buzz fades. In your early years, discipline looks unglamorous—waking up before class to write one page, finishing a side project when everyone else streams new shows, making one extra cold call. But over six or twelve months, those tiny repetitions become your builder's edge.

I once believed consistency was just for "organized" people. Turns out, it's a secret weapon for those who keep showing up when nobody's cheering. My streak of 40 consecutive days working on a personal project did more for my confidence, output, and learning than months of sporadic "all-nighters."

The Habit Loop: How Builders Widen the Gap

Cue → Routine → Reward

- Cue: A daily trigger—alarm, coffee mug, reminder note.
- Routine: The action—write 200 words, code for 30 minutes, post content, review progress.
- Reward: The payoff—small sense of achievement, a green check on your tracker, permission to brag (to yourself or your accountability buddy).

Most people only show up when inspiration strikes. Builders make showing up automatic.

Building Your Momentum Routine

1. Start Tiny: Pick one "no-brainer" builder action (making your bed, sending one pitch email, writing one idea daily).
2. Stack It: Hook your new habit to something you already do—right after chai, before the first lecture, after gym.
3. Track Publicly: Print a 30-day calendar; tick off each streak. Or, post progress in a small group chat.
4. Forgive Breaks: Missed a day? Restart, don't quit. Consistency compounds even when it's not perfect.

Action Sheet: The 21-Day Consistency Tracker

Day	Did I Show Up?	Habit Completed	Notes/Comments
1	✓ / X	Yes/No	
2	✓ / X	Yes/No	
...			
21	✓ / X	Yes/No	

- Choose your core builder habit.
- Commit for 21 days. Circle your streak, celebrate week milestones, review at the end.

Real Builder Story: Consistency Over Hype

In my second year, launching MinySite tested my patience—progress was slow, no viral moments, more rejections than wins. But by working on it 20 minutes a day, every day, my team built features that bigger competitors ignored. Clients noticed our steady upgrades, and soon, we landed our first major B2B deal—not from a marketing burst, but from months of little actions stacking into something real.

Signature Prompt: Your Momentum Mantra

"Motivation is what gets you started. Habit is what keeps you going."
— Jim Ryun

Write your own mantra for consistency in your notes or on your wall—revisit it every time you're tempted to break the streak.

Takeaway: Compounding Wins

Every ticked-off habit, every boring repetition, is a brick. Over months, those bricks build walls—walls that can support a brand, a product, a new identity. Ignore the hype; invest in consistency. It's the most underrated growth hack you'll ever find.

On the next page: Learn to manage your first money, set up real systems for young builders, and use your habits to control not just your time, but your bank account.

Part - IV
Growth & Resilience

MONEY MANAGEMENT FOR YOUNG BUILDERS

Why Early Money Habits Shape Your Destiny

Money isn't just currency—it's leverage, options, and confidence. In your teens and early twenties, the way you handle small amounts determines how you'll handle much bigger sums later. Most young builders feel "money doesn't matter until I have more"; the reality is, every financial win or misstep teaches you how to scale with discipline.

When I earned my first ₹500 online, I wasted half on impulse buys. But when I began tracking, budgeting, and setting aside even tiny profits for tools or learning (not upgrades and snacks), my hustle scaled faster. The earlier you master money, the sooner you're free to take risks, invest in yourself, and grow without fear.

The Young Builder's Money Map

1. **Track Every Rupee, Dollar, or Spend**
    - Use a simple Google Sheet, Notion page, or a pocket diary.
    - Note down every bit of income (side hustle, stipend, gifts, freelance gigs) and every expense—no matter how small.
    - Weekly review: Where is your money actually going

- Grow: 30% for savings/investing—bank FD, SIP, or digital wallet. This is your safety net and future seed fund.
- Enjoy: 30% for guilt-free spending—experiences, meals, celebration. Building is a marathon, not starvation.

1. **Avoid Lifestyle Creep**
   - Just because you earn more doesn't mean you need to spend more. Upgrade only what improves speed, health, or skill.
2. **Automate Wisely**
   - Set up auto-transfers for "grow" and "build" buckets, so you're not tempted to blow it all on a weekend sale.

Action Sheet: Young Builder's Budget Table

Income Source	This Month	% for Build	% for Grow	% for Enjoy
Freelance Coding	₹2,000	₹800	₹600	₹600
Tutoring	₹1,000	₹400	₹300	₹300
Side Hustle Profits	₹500	₹200	₹150	₹150
TOTAL	₹3,500	₹1,400	₹1,050	₹1,050

Fill in your real numbers each month and track growth over time.

Signature Prompt: Your First Investment

"It's not about how much you earn, but what you do with what you earn."

Write in your notes:

- One tool, course, or experience you'll invest in with next month's "build" fund.

- One area where you typically overspend (food delivery, gadgets, subscriptions)—set a monthly limit.
- One future goal (laptop upgrade, event fee) to save toward from your "grow" bucket.

Real Builder Story: The Power of Tiny Investments

When I budgeted my third month's earnings, I finally bought a ring light with my "build" fund—nothing fancy, but my video quality improved and so did my bookings. That one tool, bought with conscious money, paid for itself within weeks. Small, intentional spending multiplies returns.

Takeaway: Control Money, or It Controls You

Every rupee managed is a decision toward a freer, bolder builder's life. Your money is your runway. Track it, respect it, nurture it—and let it fuel the next big thing you create.

Next up: Learn modern, digital-first marketing—even before you spend a single cent on ads. Your financial discipline will multiply every effort from here.

EARLY-STAGE MARKETING — DIGITAL FIRST

Why "Digital First" Changes the Game

Forget old-school marketing that needs huge budgets, fancy banners, or citywide hoardings. Today, a single phone, a free social account, and the courage to hit "publish" can put your ideas in front of thousands—sometimes millions—of the right people, if you learn to play by digital rules. As a young builder, being "digital first" isn't about vanity—it's about speed, reach, and learning fast from real feedback.

When I began promoting my projects, I had no marketing budget. What I did have: time to DM potential users, post in relevant communities, and tell my story honestly. My first hundred downloads came not from ads, but from writing posts that spoke to student problems, joining budding founder groups on Telegram, and sharing tiny successes (and failures) online.

The Builder's Digital Marketing Stack

1. **Start With Story, Not Sales**
    - Don't sell benefits first. Tell why you built this.
    - Share behind-the-scenes: your messy desk, the late-night troubleshooting, even your first rejection.
    - Authenticity beats polish, especially with Gen Z or college users.

1. **Pick Two Digital Platforms (Master Before You Multiply)**
    - Instagram/Twitter/LinkedIn: Choose based on your target audience (students? Startups? Job-seekers?).
    - WhatsApp Groups/Telegram Channels: Goldmines for direct feedback and word-of-mouth—especially in India and SEA.
    - Post consistently: Aim for value over volume (one honest post > five copy-paste promos).

1. **Create Interactive, Action-Driven Content**
    - Polls, Q&A stickers, mini "Ask Me Anything" sessions.
    - Short explainers: Why your product solves something their friends struggle with.
    - Share testimonials, stories from first users, and the lessons behind your failures.
2. **Use Small, Trackable Challenges**
    - Launch a "7-day builder sprint" for your audience—ask users to share their work with a common hashtag or tag your handle.
    - Run a giveaway or contest: reward feedback or participation instead of random followers.
3. **DM, Comment, Collaborate**
    - Directly message five people every week—ask for advice, feedback, or help amplifying your project.
    - Leave thoughtful, useful comments on posts by bigger creators, in niche groups, or under related hashtags.

Action Sheet: Your First Digital Launch Plan

Step 1: Write your founder story in 3-5 sentences.

Step 2: Choose 2 platforms.

Step 3: Ideate and schedule three value posts for next week.

Step 4: DM five relevant people—ask for help or share your journey.
Step 5: Plan one community action (mini-challenge, live Q&A, or poll)

Platform	What I'll Share	When	Who to Tag/DM	Result to Measure
Instagram	My "why" story	Mon 8pm	3 builder friends	Comments, DMs
LinkedIn	Tips for student builders	Thu 7pm	2 college clubs, 2 mentors	Likes, shares, replies
WhatsApp Group	New offer + mini poll	Fri 1pm	5 classmates	Responses, sign-ups

Signatura Prompt: Your First Digital Footprint

"Done is better than perfect. Shared is better than secret. Digital is the fastest way to momentum."

- Screenshot the first real comment, share, or DM you get from a stranger or non-family member.
- Save it as your "first digital win" and let it fuel your next campaign.

Real Builder Story: Viral by Accident

My first post that "blew up" wasn't a how-to or tutorial. It was an honest story about failing three times before getting my first client, posted on LinkedIn at 11PM. Peers, alumni, and even teachers reshared it. It gave my young brand more credibility than any ad—because it was real.

Takeaway: Ship Publicly, Iterate Digitally

In the digital age, the fastest-growing builders are the most visible builders. Every genuine story, tip, or launch—no matter how small—plants seeds for relationships, opportunities, and compounding reach.

Start sharing today. Your “digital first” launchpad can grow faster than you imagine

Real Builder Story: Viral by Accident

My first post that “blew up” wasn’t a how-to or tutorial. It was an honest story about failing three times before getting my first client, posted on LinkedIn at 11PM. Peers, alumni, and even teachers reshared it. It gave my young brand more credibility than any ad—because it was real.

Takeaway: Ship Publicly, Iterate Digitally

In the digital age, the fastest-growing builders are the most visible builders. Every genuine story, tip, or launch—no matter how small—plants seeds for relationships, opportunities, and compounding reach.

Start sharing today. Your “**digital first**” launchpad can grow faster than you imagine. in "**Start sharing today.** Your 'digital first' launchpad can..."

Next up: You’ll harness your digital growth—and personal story—**to build a personal brand that opens doors for years to come. Get ready for your next level.**

BUILDING A PERSONAL BRAND

Why Personal Branding Starts Early

In a world of endless noise and competition, your personal brand is the reputation you build—online and offline—long before most people notice what you're creating. For young builders, the earlier you take control of your digital story, the easier it becomes to open doors, attract opportunities, and turn chance encounters into lasting value.
I was hesitant at first—Who would care? Won't I sound braggy? But as soon as I started sharing my journey (failures, learnings, and little wins) on LinkedIn and Instagram, new connections, collaborations, and even my first speaking gig followed. Your story, honestly told, is your superpower.

Personal Branding Isn't Just Logo and Colors
It's your story.
It's your values.
It's the consistent evidence of your work and growth.

The best personal brands:

- Are authentic (they share struggles and small progress, not just highlight reels)
- Focus on serving and inspiring others, not just self-promotion
- Evolve with you, reflecting every new skill or pivot

Your Online Presence: Audit and Action

1. Google Yourself:

Search your full name. What shows up? Is it what you want future partners, clients, or employers to see? If the answer is "no" or "nothing," you have an opportunity

2.Audit Your Social Platforms:

- LinkedIn: Have a decent photo, a headline that shows what you build or strive for ("Student Entrepreneur | Digital Marketer | Web3 Learner").
- Instagram/X/Twitter: Add a one-line bio about what excites you ("Learning in public. Building @SiddInfotech.").

3. Build a Small Portfolio Site:

It can be as simple as a free Carrd.co page, Notion portfolio, or a one-page blog showing:

- Who you are
- What you're learning/building
- Three things you're proud of
- How to contact you

4. Share with Consistency:

- Post once a week: an insight, a learning, a mini-win, or a question.
- Comment actively and provide value in other communities or peer posts

.Action Sheet: Personal Brand Audit

Platform	Profile Picture	Bio Updated	Recent Share	Room for Growth
LinkedIn	✓/X	✓/X	✓/X	Notes
Instagram	✓/X	✓/X	✓/X	Notes
Portfolio	✓/X	✓/X	✓/X	Notes

Circle "✓" where you feel confident; "✗" where you need to update. Make a plan to fill those gaps in the next 7 days.

Signature Prompt: Brand in a Sentence

"If a stranger found your profile or site for the first time, what's the one thing they'd know for sure?"

Write your "brand in a sentence" and pin it in your bio, portfolio, or on your wall.

Real Builder Insight: How Personal Brand Opens Doors

Two months after I started posting weekly reflections and product updates, a local entrepreneur reached out to collaborate. He found me through a shared comment thread, not an advertisement. Your "digital footprint" is a planting ground—tiny moments, shown consistently, that attract new chances to build, earn, and connect.

Takeaway: Your Brand = Your Opportunity Magnet

Brands are built by the stories you share and the value you give, long before anyone knows your name. You don't need a million followers—start with a clear, honest bio, a small site, and weekly proof that you're learning in public.

Control your narrative. Build a reputation you're proud of.

On the next page: You'll learn how to navigate failure, use feedback as fuel, and make your brand truly resilient—even when things go "wrong."

Failing Forward – Embracing Mistakes and Feedback

Why Failure Is Fuel (Not a Finish Line)

We're taught to avoid mistakes, to fear red marks, to equate "failure" with the end of the story. But every real builder you admire has failed—often more times than you'll ever know.

What separates lasting creators from the rest is not that their plans never flopped, but that they learned, adapted, and built again—wiser each time.

Early in my journey, I dreaded mistakes. My first website crashed on launch day. A digital product went weeks with zero sales. I flopped on stage during a college hackathon pitch. Each time felt like public defeat. Yet, every time I got honest feedback—sometimes harsh, sometimes kind—it pointed the way to my next win.

The Four Stages of Failing Forward

1. Shock and Sting
    - It hurts. It's frustrating. Don't sugarcoat it. Write down what happened—describing it makes the pain smaller and the lesson clearer.
2. Analysis Without Excuses
    - Ask: What went wrong? Was it poor planning, overconfidence, lack of research, or skipping real feedback?
    - Pro tip: Externalize the blame for a few minutes, then own your piece.

3. Harvest the Lesson
    - What specific action will you take differently next time?
    - Even a single sentence ("Next time, I'll test with 3 users before launching") is gold.
4. Share and Move On
    - Sharing your story builds trust. Others see that you're learning, not hiding—and sometimes, they jump in with wisdom or support

Real Story: My First Business Setback

Sidd Infotech's brand logo service seemed bulletproof—until a rushed project missed a client's big event. I saw my first refund request and a public review that stung: "Fast, friendly, but missed the mark."

I wanted to shrink away. Instead, I called the client, apologized, asked detailed questions, and offered a free fix—which led to a positive update and a referral two months later. That one failure taught me to communicate openly and never overpromise on deadlines.

Feedback as Your Fastest Growth Engine

- Seek active feedback from users, mentors, or even critics.
- "What didn't work or you?" is sometimes more valuable than "What did?"
- Create a "Red Flag" list after every project—mistakes, overlooked details, poor bets.
- Review that list before your next launch. Spot patterns, double-check where you often slip.

Action Sheet: Failure Reflection Table

Failure or Setback	What I Felt	Lesson Learned	Action for Next Time
Missed client deadline	Embarrassment, guilt	Clarify workload, double-check ETA	Schedule buffer days, update client more often
Zero course signups	Frustration	Need better audience research	Survey 10 potential users before building
Unread pitch emails	Rejection	Subject line too generic	Personalize opening line, research recipients

- Fill in your own "small or big" failures from this year.

Signature Prompt: The Failure Vault

"Each mistake you own becomes a future shortcut. Scars are proof that you're building in the real world."

Write this mantra somewhere visible:
"My next win will grow from my last mistake."

Takeaway: Builders Are Forged in Setbacks

If you haven't failed this month, you may not be aiming high enough. Embrace feedback. Learn out loud. Treat each flop as a tuition payment for your real education in the building game.
When you stop hiding from mistakes and start mining them for gold, you move from fearing failure to failing forward—and that's the difference-maker for every extraordinary journey.

Next up: How to keep building momentum—and finding resourceful, creative ways forward—even when you have zero funding or connections.

BUILDING WITHOUT FUNDING OR CONNECTIONS

The "Bootstrap Builder" Reality

The most common excuse I hear from young dreamers is: "I'd start if I had funding," or, "I don't know the right people." The truth? Most legendary builders you admire—especially in tech and startups—began with empty pockets and only a handful of friends who believed (or sometimes, none at all).

You don't need a rich uncle, VC backing, or glamorous network to make momentum real

When I launched my first project, my monthly "budget" was a few hundred rupees, often borrowed. I used free tools, worked from shared rooms, and learned to turn every setback into a workaround. Scarcity taught me creativity—and every ounce of progress meant more because I earned it, piece by piece.

The Bootstrap Blueprint: How to Build with Little (or No) Money

1. Leverage Free and "Freemium" Tools
    - Website builders (Carrd, Notion, Google Sites)
    - Free logo and graphic tools (Canva, Figma)
    - Free Google Workspace, WhatsApp, Telegram

- Free Google Workspace, WhatsApp, Telegram for collaboration/marketing
- Free learning (YouTube, open online courses, Reddit communities)

1. Barter & Skill Swap
   - Offer your design, code, or writing skills to peers in exchange for help (copy editing, intro calls, social sharing)
   - Join student entrepreneurship cells, local business clubs; pitch a "let's trade skills" challenge
2. Build in Public
   - Share your learning, failures, and process on platforms like LinkedIn, Twitter, or Reddit
   - Document as you go—people are more likely to help and amplify your work if they see you're consistent and transparent
3. Turn Small "Wins" Into Social Proof
   - Screenshot every bit of positive feedback, DM, test user
   - Ask your first clients for testimonials, tags, or "shout-outs" no matter how informal
4. Find Micro-mentors
   - DM recent grads, local entrepreneurs, or rising creators (not just "famous" names)—ask a single, specific question, not for partnership or money
   - Show what you're working on in your outreach, not just what you want.

Personal Story: Learning to Out-Resource Resourcefulness

When cash ran out, I borrowed an old Android phone to shoot content. To get my first 10 users, I hosted a free digital "workshop" in a college lab, promising a Canva template in exchange for honest feedback. With every "no" from an investor or potential partner, I asked myself: "What's my zero-budget alternative?"

Someday you might have capital or name recognition—but your box-of-tools approach during the scrappy stage will always serve you

Action Sheet: Bootstrap Building Planner

Need/Goal	Free/Freemium Tool or Resource Used	Who Can Help/Barter?	My "Zero-Rupee" Tactic
Host a website	Carrd.co, Notion	Coding club peer	Swap help for Canva designs
Social promo	Instagram, LinkedIn free posts	Classmate with reach	Shout-out in exchange for editing
Learning marketing	YouTube, HubSpot Academy	Mentor in WhatsApp group	DM with specific question

- Fill this table for your current project or hustle.
- List every "I can't afford" item and brainstorm two alternatives—one digital, one relationship-based.

Signature Prompt: The "Zero-Excuse" Builder Pledge

"The best builders learn to do more with less—until doing more with more is easy."

Write this in your notes:

- What's the #1 thing you believe you can't build without money or connections?
- What's your scrappy alternative?
- Who will you share your progress with, so they can be part of your journey?

Key Takeaway: Relentless Resourcefulness Wins

No one hands you momentum. You earn it, especially in the years when you have little money, few contacts, and only your next idea burning in your pocket.

Your "bootstrap" stage builds two irreplaceable assets: creativity (making much from little) and humility (valuing every ally and every lesson, however small).

Build with what you have, where you are—doors you can't see now will swing open as you move.

Next: ***Learn how to turn critics, doubts, and fears into tools for growth—building even when you feel alone or stuck. The real builder's journey continues.***

Managing Fear, Criticism, and Inner Resistance

Why Fear Is a Builder's Constant Companion

Fear isn't a sign you're not ready—it's a signal you're on the edge of real growth. Every builder, no matter how successful, battles self-doubt, nerves, and the internal voice that whispers, "What if I'm not good enough?" The trick isn't to eliminate fear or silence criticism—it's to build despite them.

When I posted my first product online, I was terrified of ridicule: "What if nobody buys? What if people laugh? Will friends think I'm showing off?" What actually happened? A few silent days, a message from a kind stranger, and eventually, real feedback—some helpful, plenty confusing, and one comment that stung: "Looks amateur." But inside that pain, I found the motivation to improve.

Three Types of Criticism and How to Use Them

1. Constructive
    - Comes from those who care (mentors, users, honest peers).
    - Action: Thank them, clarify what's unclear, implement the advice.
2. Destructive/Jealous
    - Mean-spirited, vague, or rooted in someone else's insecurity

- Action: Ignore the tone, salvage any useful detail, block the rest.

1. Your Own Inner Voice
    - Often the harshest—"Are you sure?" "What if this fails again?"
    - Action: Write down your fears; name them. Doubt shrinks in the light.

Taming Inner Resistance: The 3-Minute Rule

Anytime you feel paralyzed by fear, do this:

- Write down the exact thing you're scared will happen (e.g., "People will laugh at my video").
- List one thing you'd do if that happened (e.g., "Ask a mentor for honest feedback, improve, try again").
- Set a timer for 3 minutes and start on your next task—don't wait for confidence, let action trigger momentum

.

Action Sheet: Criticism Convert Table

Criticism/Fear	Source	Truth in It?	Action I'll Take
"Feels amateur"	Online comment	Needs better design	Watch two design tutorials, update
"Nobody's interested"	Inner voice	No messages?	DM ten people for feedback
"What if I fail again?"	Own thoughts	Possible, but...	Re-read my failure lessons, try again

Fill this in after you launch or share something new.

Signature Prompt: The "Public Flop" Story

"If you never fail in public, you're not aiming high enough to matter."

Real Builder Story: Criticism That Changed My Path

During my first college startup fair, a judge dismissed my pitch with, "You're too young to understand the market." I felt crushed—old insecurities came roaring back. Instead of quitting, I emailed the judge, asked for a second chance to explain, and discovered holes in my research. The next iteration won a local prize, and the feedback I feared led me to prepare 10x better for my real audience.

Key Takeaway: Courage Practiced Daily

You don't rise above fear once and for all; you build calluses by acting with it, every day. Builders who put themselves out there fail more publicly, but they also learn and improve much faster.

- Transform criticism into your next breakthrough.
- Use fear as the "green light" that you're moving into meaningful territory.
- Make a habit of shipping before you're sure.

On the next page: Discover how to find mentors, build networks from scratch, and turn simple outreach into relationships that fuel your journey for years ahead. This is where you stop building alone.

FINDING MENTORS & BUILDING NETWORKS

Why You Can't Build Alone

Every great builder—no matter how "self-made"—rose faster with a little outside help. Mentorship and supportive networks aren't shortcuts; they're rocket fuel. You don't need celebrity investors or an uncle in venture capital. The real network starts with a handful of people who've walked your path, are a few steps ahead, or simply believe in action.

When I sought my first mentor, I felt intimidated. But it was a direct (nervous) DM to a local entrepreneur, not a big-name startup star, that changed everything. He reviewed my project, offered honest feedback, and pointed me to my first batch of paying users. That early support saved me months—if not years—of searching in the dark.

Types of Mentors (and Where to Find Them)

1. Peer Mentors
    - Classmates, fellow builders, or teammates facing similar challenges.
    - Tip: Form a WhatsApp/Messenger group: "Accountability Partners" for daily or weekly check-ins.

- Near-Peer Mentors
  - Recent graduates, young professionals, alumni, or those 1–3 years ahead.
  - Tip: Scan LinkedIn, college alumni groups, or Slack channels; reach out with: "I admire your work on ___. Can I ask 2 quick questions about your journey?"

How to Reach Out & Build Relationships

- **Be specific and respectful**: Instead of "Will you be my mentor?" try, "I'm launching my first project and struggling with X. Could you share any advice or resources?"
- **Show you're a builder**: Mention something you've already created or tested. People love helping doers, not just dreamers.
- **Follow up (but don't pester):** If you get advice, use it, and report back on your progress. Most mentors rarely receive updates—and will remember you as the rare action-taker.

Building Networks from the Ground Up

- **Join and participate actively:** Local entrepreneurship cells, online communities (Discords, FB groups, industry forums), college societies.
- **Give before you ask:** Share helpful resources, answer beginner questions, help promote others' work.
- **Attend events (offline or online):** Volunteer at conferences or hackathons—relationships built behind-the-scenes often outlast those formed during formal networking.

Action Sheet: Mentor & Network Builder Plan

1. List 3–5 specific people (by name / profile) you want to connect with this month.
2. Draft your short, respectful outreach message:

"Hi [Name], I admire your journey in [area]. I'm working on [project]. Could I ask a quick question about [topic]?
"

3.Identify two networks or groups to join and one way you can contribute (post, share, answer, organize).

Name/Network	Role (Peer/Expert)	Outreach Plan	Follow-Up Action
Example: Priya (alum)	Near-Peer	LinkedIn DM	Share project update
Example: Startup Hub	Group	Attend weekly call	Share helpful tool

Signature Prompt: "The First Ask"

"The right mentor may be one honest message away—but you have to make the first move."

Write down:

- Who will you reach out to this week?
- What question or specific help do you need?
- How will you prove you acted on advice, not just collected it?

Real Builder Story: A Mentor's Ripple Effect

When I stayed late at a free local marketing workshop, the organizer (a young marketer) noticed me—scribbling detailed notes, asking questions after the session. A month later, she referred me to a freelance gig that paid for my new laptop. Years later, we co-hosted events and swapped referrals as friends and collaborators. One reach-out led to a career-changing ripple.

Key Takeaway: Community Multiplies Builders

Even the smallest network is a multiplier: for ideas, courage, introductions, and opportunity. Mentors open doors that skill alone cannot; communities become your ongoing source of advice, collaboration, and momentum when you hit walls.

On the next page: You'll put this new network into practice, stepping into your first 100-day action blueprint—with support, feedback, and **unstoppable momentum.**

You are never building alone

Chapter : V (Multiply and Sustain)

THE FIRST 100 DAYS — STEP-BY-STEP BLUEPRINT

Why 100 Days Can Change Everything

The distance between idea and real momentum is often just 100 intentional days. Most young builders underestimate how much they can shift their trajectory in a focused season. Your next 3 months can lay foundations for skills, confidence, and results that compound for years—if you act with bold clarity and structured goals.

I challenged myself to a "100-day builder sprint" during my second year of college. The rules were simple: show up daily, track progress, refine my projects, and share at least one insight a week. The discipline, wins, and relationships built in that period became the engine of my entire journey.

The 100-Day Builder Blueprint

1. **Set One Bold Goal**
    - Identify the highest-impact project, skill, or offer you want to build or launch (e.g., ship your first digital product, reach 50 paying customers, learn a new code stack, or launch a personal brand).
    - Write it down publicly: notebook, sticky note, or Instagram Story. Social commitment increases follow-through

2. **Break the 100 Days Into 4 Sprints**

- Sprint 1 (Days 1–25): Deep dive. Learn, map, and prototype. Fast experiments over perfect planning.
- Sprint 2 (Days 26–50): First public launch or share. Feedback loop—collect reviews, adjust, improve.
- Sprint 3 (Days 51–75): Scale and systemize. Reach for more users, automate daily tasks, teach one thing you learned to someone else.
- Sprint 4 (Days 76–100): Measure and multiply. Review results, iterate, record lessons. Prepare the next version or graduation project based on what worked.

3. Create a Daily Tracker

Day	Action/Check-in	Win/Challenge	Hours Invested	Notes/Reflection
1				
2				
…				
100				

- Record something every day—progress, pivots, failures, even doubts. The log itself becomes proof of growth.

4. Weekly Reflection & Public Sharing

Once a week, write a short update (on social, in a group chat, or even a private diary):

- What was the one biggest win?
- Where did you get stuck, and what did you learn?
- What's the next experiment or step for the coming week?

5. Seek Accountability

Pair up with another builder, invite feedback from a mentor, or join an online "100-day challenge" group. Shared visibility multiplies motivation.

Signature Prompt: Your 100-Day Commitment

"A hundred small actions are worth more than one big intention."

- Write today's date and your Day 1 goal.
- List who will hold you accountable.
- What will you celebrate at Day 100—regardless of the outcome?

Real Builder Insight: Why Sprints > Waiting

During my first 100-day sprint, I failed to hit my revenue goal. But I built two new products, doubled my following, and learned more in three months than the previous two years. The challenge wasn't about perfection—it was about building the muscle of daily commitment. That habit has powered every leap since.

Takeaway: Build Momentum Out Loud

The world favors those who show up. Your 100-day sprint will not just change your skillset—it will change who you believe you are. The next page will help you scale your experiments and transform wins (and stumbles) into a system for true growth.

You're 100 days away from a new story. Start the count

Scaling Up – From Mini-Project to Startup

Why Scaling Changes the Game

Building your first project or making a small side income is thrilling—but the leap from "mini-project" to a sustainable startup is where you truly evolve as a builder. Scaling isn't just about growing user numbers or revenue—it's about designing repeatable systems, automating what works, and learning to let go of what slows you down.

I remember turning Sidd Infotech from a late-night WhatsApp experiment into a registered company. Suddenly, every decision—hiring, legal setup, brand voice, cash flow—had higher stakes. It was overwhelming at first, but every challenge became a lesson in focus, delegation, and vision

The Scaling Blueprint

1. **Document What Works**
    - For every task you repeat—outreach, onboarding, project delivery—write a simple checklist or workflow.
    - Example: A template for client emails, a standard process for releases, a Google Sheet for financial tracking.

1. Automate or Delegate
    - Use free or affordable tools:
        - Automate invoices, emails (Zapier, Google Workspace)
        - Schedule social posts (Buffer, Hootsuite)
        - Use simple bots for support queries or feedback collection
    - When overwhelmed, bring in a partner, a freelancer, or even a junior with one clear responsibility.
2. Customer Feedback Loops
    - As your audience or client base grows, set up regular feedback check-ins: surveys, WhatsApp polls, review requests.
    - Learn which features, content, or services spark loyalty or referrals—and double down on these.
3. Financial Systems for Growth
    - Open a dedicated bank or digital wallet for your startup/hustle.
    - Separate business and personal expenses, track all inflows/outflows weekly.
    - As revenue grows, consider basic legalities: GST registration, company incorporation, simple contracts.
4. Identity Shift: From Hustler to Founder
    - Change your inner dialogue: you are building a business, not just "trying" an idea.
    - Communicate this vision to your team, users, and—crucially—yourself. This reframing unlocks new discipline and confidence.

Action Sheet: Scaling Self-Assessment

Area	Current Status	Next System/Tool	Target Date
Client Onboarding	Manual messages	Automated email sequence	7 days
Feedback Process	Ad-hoc WhatsApp	Google Form survey	This week
Social Media	Posts by hand	Buffer schedule	Next Monday
Payments/Finance	Cash/UPI mixed	Dedicated business wallet	1 month

Fill this table for your own project and set a timeline for each upgrade.

Signature Prompt: The "Founder's Gate"

"A side project makes you resourceful. Scaling it makes you a founder."

Write down:

- What system or tool will set your project up for its next 10x growth?
- Who can you ask for help—mentor, freelancer, or peer builder?
- What single area (client experience, marketing, finance, delivery) is your biggest bottleneck right now

Real Builder Story: The Power of Systems

Scaling MinySite meant I could no longer answer every DM personally. I created FAQs, automated onboarding, and recruited a classmate to handle support. The result? Smooth launches, more time for creative work, and happier users. That step transformed a scrappy project into a brand people trusted.

Takeaway: Scale to Last

Your first rupee proves you can earn. Your first system proves you can grow.

Don't chase everything—improve what's working, cut what's slowing you down, and let simple, scalable processes become your best employee.

Turn the page: ***Ready to amplify your growth by sharing your story, teaching—and multiplying your impact beyond your product. Let's build your next level, together***

Writing, Speaking, Sharing Your Story

Why Your Story Matters—Even Before You "Make It"

Every builder's journey becomes infinitely more impactful, visible, and valuable when you learn to tell your own story. You don't need to wait for a "big win" or international recognition to start sharing. Transparency about your journey—failures, pivots, experiments, and small wins—doesn't just build your brand; it inspires and educates those a few steps behind you.

When I hesitated to write about my awkward first launch or nervous hackathon pitch, I worried, "Who am I to share?" But after one raw LinkedIn post, DMs poured in from students facing the same fears. My inbox filled not with job offers, but with new energy, ideas, and even peers who later became collaborators. Your ongoing story is one of the strongest magnets for mentorship, feedback, and reputation.

How to Write, Speak, and Teach as You Build

1. Writing (Blog, Social Posts, Digital Journals)
    - Share weekly project updates, "lessons from failure," or simple checklists.
    - Use real numbers and honest timelines ("I failed three times before landing my first sale").

- Include a "builder's takeaway" in every post: one line others can use or share.

Speaking (Workshops, Panels, Live Streams)

- Start small: Class presentations, department webinars, or IG Lives.
- Frame your talk around "what I wish I knew before..." rather than what makes you an expert.
- Offer one actionable idea or practical tool per session.

3. Teaching and Sharing Templates
   - Convert your best checklists, pitch decks, or audit sheets into downloadable templates (Google Docs, Notion pages).
   - Invite feedback, encourage others to remix or improve them.
   - List these resources on personal sites or during talks—each tool shared increases your reach and authority.

Action Sheet: Story Sharing Plan

Format	Topic/Angle	Audience	Where to Share	Frequency
Blog Post	"My First Startup Flop"	Student builders	Medium, LinkedIn	Monthly
Instagram Carousel	"3 Hard Truths I Learned"	Gen Z, creators	Instagram	Weekly
Campus Webinar	"Building Without Funding"	College societies	WhatsApp, Zoom	Quarterly
Resource Template	100-Day Planner	Early builders	Notion, Google Docs	Ongoing

- Fill in your own plan for page 30 and beyond!

Signature Prompt: Share Before "Success"

"The world is waiting for honest journeys, not perfect ones."

Choose one story from your journey—however awkward, painful, or unfinished. Write a post, record a short video, or teach a quick session.

Ask:

- What did I struggle with? How did I move forward?
- What's one thing I learned that could help someone else start?

Real Builder Story: The Ripple Effect of an Honest Post

One of my most-shared posts was about nearly giving up after a stretch of "invisible" work—late nights, no users, a rejected pitch. The unexpected messages: "This is exactly what I needed to hear!" "I'm in month six and was about to quit."

Your vulnerability not only makes you relatable—it connects you to people who could become friends, clients, and fans for life.

Takeaway: Teach as You Go

Don't wait until you're "qualified" or have a viral story. The act of writing, speaking, and teaching cements your learnings, attracts your network, and multiplies your impact

—years before your product or project gets big. Remember, your unfinished chapters today are the survival guides for someone else's tomorrow

on the next page: You'll discover 10 powerful lessons that shaped my journey before 21—real stories to keep you building and believing, even when the world says it's impossible.

LESSONS BEFORE 21 – TOP 10 STORIES THAT SHAPED ME

Why Stories Matter More Than Tips

Real change happens through moments, not just advice. Here, I'm sharing 10 pivotal stories—each one a fork in my builder's road, with the lessons, doubts, and little wins that changed everything. These aren't highlight reels, but unfiltered snapshots: failures, unexpected breaks, risky decisions, and the tiny actions that led to big growth.

Lesson 1: The Day I Sent the First Cold Email

Story:

I typed and retyped a simple request for feedback. Hands trembling, I hit send to a local business owner—and got an unexpected reply an hour later: "Come for chai, let's talk."

Lesson: Take the first step even if you don't feel ready. Most opportunities are one honest DM away.

Lesson 2: My Worst Hackathon Pitch

Story:

Fumbled slides, shaky voice—my idea got silence, then a single, blunt suggestion from a judge. I rewrote my pitch, returned next time, and placed second.

Lesson: Feedback that stings is often the one that points to your real growth gap.

Lesson 3: Earning My First ₹500 Online

Story:

Selling digital notes to classmates, I discovered belief follows action—not the other way around. That payment alert was my turning point.

Lesson: Small wins break big doubts—take any action that creates real feedback from the market.

Lesson 4: Investing in a Course (Instead of an Upgrade)

Story:

Skipped a smartphone upgrade, bought a copywriting course that led to my first freelance client.

Lesson: Invest in skills before stuff—knowledge multiplies; gadgets only depreciate.

Lesson 5: The Burnout Scare

Story:

Said "yes" to everything; ended up exhausted and unproductive. Only after setting non-negotiable boundaries did quality and momentum return.

Lesson: Protect your energy as fiercely as you chase new projects.

Lesson 6: First Team, First Disagreement

Story

My first collaborators quit over task confusion. We had never set roles or expectations.

Lesson: Clarity in communication makes or breaks teams—always define "who does what, by when."

Lesson 7: Posting My "Fail" Online

Story:

Publicly shared that my product flopped. Received advice, encouragement, and even a future cofounder in my DMs.

Lesson: Vulnerability attracts your tribe—don't hide your mistakes.

Lesson 8: The "No Money? Build Anyway" Decision

Story:

No capital meant leveraging free tools and offering free trials to first customers. The constraint sparked unexpected creativity.

Lesson: Resourcefulness grows faster than resources ever will.

Lesson 9: Standing My Ground With a Client

Story:

Refused to lower my freelance rate below what felt fair. Lost the deal, but gained my self-respect and better projects later.

Lesson: Respect your value—even if it means saying "no" before you can fully afford to.

Lesson 10: Paying It Forward

Story:

Mentored a younger student for free, helping him avoid a few landmines I hit. His gratitude—and results—rekindled my own momentum

Lessons: The fastest way to break through ruts is to help someone else climb higher.

Signature Prompt: Craft Your "First 10" List

Jot down 10 moments—good, bad, or quietly formative—since you first thought about "building."

- What did you learn?
- How did it change your next action?

Stories make lessons stick. Your first ten will guide your next hundred.

Takeaway:

You don't need decades to become "experienced"—just 10 true lessons, lived with honesty, reflected on with care, and applied again and again.

Your next story starts on the following page. Make it unforgettable.

The Next Decade – Your 10-Year Compass

Why You Need a Long-View—Even Before 21

Legendary builders aren't defined by one viral project or lucky break. Their secret? Playing the long game. When you craft a 10-year vision—even if it shifts along the way—you stop obsessing over daily noise, setbacks, or FOMO. Instead, you set direction, make better choices, and learn to weather storms other quit in.

During my first years as a builder, I had only hazy dreams. But outlining where I wanted to be at 28—not just in career, but in habits, relationships, and impact—became my secret weapon. That compass made every "small" day meaningful, and every setback just one frame in a bigger story.

The 10-Year Vision Map

1. **Start With the End in Mind**
    - Where do you want your life to be in 10 years?
        - What are you building?
        - Who are you helping?
        - What skills and relationships define your growth?
2. **Break It Down: The 3 Pillars**
    - Skill Stack: What new abilities will you master? (Think: not just technical, but leadership, communication, creativity)

- Impact: What legacy, project, or community will outlast you?
- Lifestyle: What does your ideal day look like—work, health, family, freedom?

3.Reverse-Engineer Milestones

- Year 10: Where do you want to reach?
- Year 5: What would be halfway there?
- Year 3: What must you've started by then?
- Year 1: What will you launch or build in the next 12 months?

Action Sheet: Crafting Your Decade Compass

Year	Skill/Project	Impact/Legacy	Lifestyle/Well-Being	Notes/Checkpoint
1	Launch first e-product	Help 50+ students	Morning creator habit	1 client/month
3	Start startup/Side biz	Mentor peers	Flex work hours	Speak at event
5	Scale team/brand	Start social project	Fitness, more family time	Write a book
10	Lead own company, invest in others	Community programs	Purpose-led life, global travels	"Big impact" goals

- Sketch your own. Start with a rough draft; the picture sharpens over time.

Signature Prompt: Write a Letter to Your Future Self

"The most powerful thing you can do is plant a flag far ahead, so you're never lost in the noise of daily setbacks."

- Address it: "Dear [Your Name], age 28..."
- Describe what you hope you've experienced, built, given—and the non-negotiable habits or values you hope you stuck with.
- Seal or save it somewhere visible. Revisit yearly

Real Builder Example: My 10-Year Compass

When I mapped out "Tanweer—2025," my goals included:

- Running a profitable, impact-first business.
- Mentoring young founders, especially in small towns.
- Traveling to 10 countries.
- Practicing creative routines daily.

Years later, not all goals came true in the way I imagined—but each choice, project, and routine became easier, guided by a future-me I was determined to meet.

Takeaway: Your Decade, Your Design

You won't control every outcome. Life will twist, test, and surprise you. But with a 10-year compass, you'll drift less, rebound faster, and build a legacy—one honest step at a time.

Ready for the next phase? On the following page, you'll find the conclusion—a final wake-up plan to keep your momentum strong, long after the last page. Your real journey is only beginning.

CONCLUSION – YOUR WAKE-UP ACTION PLAN

The End Is Just Your Beginning

Congratulations—by reaching this page, you've joined the rare 5% who finish what they start. But the real prize isn't information; it's ignition. The years ahead aren't just blank pages…they're an open field for every risk, experiment, mistake, and win you choose to create. Your "Build Before 21" journey isn't about doing everything right the first time—it's about moving, learning, and refusing to stay on the sidelines.

Years ago, I finished my first business book and closed the cover, inspired…but unchanged. This book is designed differently. If all you do is read, progress stops here. The world only changes when builders act.

Your Wake-Up Action Plan

1. Pick One Chapter, One Exercise

Don't try to master it all at once. Go back to the chapter that stung, excited, or challenged you most. Complete the action sheet, worksheet, or prompt again—with your future self in mind.

2. Set a 7-Day Builder Sprint

Decide today:

- One skill, side hustle, or routine you'll begin this week.

- Where you'll track your streak (journal, calendar, group chat).
- Share your goal with one trusted friend or public post—accountability multiplies odds.

3. Find Your Accountability Tribe

Message a friend, join an online group, or DM me personally. Declare: "I'm building before [your next birthday/semester/new year]." Invite others to join. Builders build better in community.

4. Schedule Monthly Self-Reviews

Every 30 days, reflect:

- Where did I take action?
- What did I learn (even from failure)?
- What's my next "first step"?

Use your builder's log, audit table, or even voice notes—make progress visible.

Signature Statement: Your "I'm a Builder" Declaration

"Today, I choose action over analysis, imperfect starts over perfect intentions, and a decade of building over a lifetime of waiting. The next page is blank—but it's mine to fill."

Sign. Date. Snap a photo. Carry it as a reminder that you don't need permission—only commitment

Final Builder's Blessing

May your next side project flop, just so you learn resilience.

May your first client praise your grit, not just your work.

May your circle multiply with collaborators, cheerleaders, and future mentors.

And may your twenties—and every decade after—echo with the impact of the future you started building now.

Thank you for trusting your journey with me. I can't wait to see, share, and celebrate what you create.

— Tanweer Sidd

[On the next page: *Explore resources, templates, and tools to keep your momentum alive. The building never ends—it only levels up.*]

Resources & Appendices

RESOURCE LIST – KEEP BUILDING, KEEP WINNING

Why You Need a Go-To Resource Toolkit

The builders who keep momentum don't just rely on willpower or talent—they assemble (and revisit) a toolkit of trusted resources. Whether you hit a wall or want to scale up, knowing where to look saves months and multiplies every effort. This resource list is your starter pack, curated from the most game-changing tools, platforms, and learning sites from my own journey.

Essential Learning Platforms

- **YouTube**

Master everything—from coding to copywriting to digital art.
Favorite channels: Traversy Media, Abhi and Niyu, Ali Abdaal (productivity/life skills).

- **Coursera, edX, and Khan Academy**

Free and university-backed courses for skills from basics to advanced.

- **Google Digital Garage**

Free certifications in analytics, digital marketing, and professional communication.

Tools for Builders & Hustlers

- **Canva**

Instantly create pro-level social posts, decks, and brand materials.

- **Notion, Google Docs, Sheets**

Organize your projects and create living knowledge bases—templates for audit sheets, trackers, pitch decks.

- **Carrd, Wix, Google Sites**

Build quick, beautiful websites or portfolio landing pages at zero or low cost.

- **Zapier, Buffer, Hootsuite**

Automate content scheduling, email sequences, data flows.

Find Your Community

- **Reddit:** r/Entrepreneur, r/IndiaStartups, r/Productivity for crowd wisdom.
- **Discord/WhatsApp Groups:** Search by niche ("student founders," "digital creators India," campus innovation cells).
- **LinkedIn / Twitter (X):** Connect to creators, mentors—search by hashtags (#BuildInPublic, #YoungEntrepreneur, #DigitalIndia).

Extra Fuel: Inspiration & Skill Growth

- **Podcasts**:
  - The Tim Ferriss Show
  - Masters of Scale by Reid Hoffman

- STAGE by Tanmay Bhat (for Indian creators/founders)

- **Books**:
  - Atomic Habits by James Clear (habits, compounding wins)
  - Show Your Work! by Austin Kleon (how sharing leads to growth)
  - The Lean Startup by Eric Ries (minimum viable product, fast launching)

Downloadables and Templates

- 100-Day Builder Planner: Notion and printable PDF versions (available via link or DM/email in the appendices).
- Audit Sheet Template: Plug-and-play Google Sheet from the earlier chapter.
- Pitch Deck & Email Scripts: Free downloads listed on my portfolio site (details in the Appendix).

Signature Prompt: Curate, Don't Hoard

"A resource untested is just a distraction. Choose three from this list, and put them into action this week."

Write down:

- One platform to learn a new skill.
- One tool to systematize your next project.
- One community where you'll contribute, not just consume

Keep updating your toolkit as you grow—your next breakthrough may be a link, message, or connection away.

On the following pages: You'll find ready-to-use templates, worksheets, and invitations to connect with a growing Build Before 21 community—to make your journey easier, faster, and never lonely. The building never stops—equip yourself, and keep leveling up!

TEMPLATE VAULT – PLUG-AND-PLAY FOR BUILDERS

Why Templates Accelerate Your Growth

Don't reinvent the wheel every time you launch, pitch, or track progress. Smart builders rely on templates—cheat codes that save hours, reduce overwhelm, and help you focus on the work that matters most. The following slice of my own Template Vault includes the actual scripts and frameworks that shaped every major leap in my journey. Use them, remix them, and share them with your builder friends.

1.**Cold Email Script**

Use for collaborating, pitching, seeking mentorship, or reaching out for feedback.

Subject: [Short, Specific Reason – e.g., "Quick Question from a Student Builder"]

Body:

Hi [Name],

I'm [Your Name], a student/young builder who's working on [short description]. I admired your work on [something specific], and wanted to ask a quick question:

[Short, direct ask or question.]

Grateful for even 1–2 lines of advice—promise to keep it short!

Thank you,

[Your Name]

[Link to LinkedIn, portfolio, or project]

2. Project Kick-Off Checklist

- Idea/Problem Statement (1 line)
- Outcome/Goal (quantifiable: "Reach 50 users in 30 days")
- Resources/Skills Needed
- Timeline (start/end dates)
- First 3 action steps
- Accountability partner/team

3. Progress Tracker Table

Date	Task/Step	Status (✅/⏳/❌)	Notes/Learnings
29/7/25	Launched landing page	✅	First 10 signups!
...			

4. Weekly Reflection Prompt

- What was this week's biggest win?
- What obstacle did I face (and how did I respond)?
- What lesson or tweak will I apply next week?
- Who did I help or connect with?

5. Feedback Request Script

Hi [Name],

I'm working on [project/skill], and value your perspective.

- What worked well?
- What was confusing or could improve?
- Anything missing you'd like to see?
- Thank you—your input helps me build better!

Signature Prompt: Build Your Own Vault

"Templates aren't shortcuts—they're springboards for speed and sanity. Improve and personalize them every time you build."

- Pick or adapt at least one template above and put it to work this week.
- Create a "Template Vault" folder in your drive or notebook—expand it as you launch, pitch, and grow.

The best builders are systems thinkers.

Your template vault is one of your most valuable assets—never build from scratch if you can build smart.

On the next page: Join the Build Before 21 community, connect directly with fellow action-takers, and share your journey for real-time support and collaboration. You're never building alone!

COMMUNITY INVITATION – JOIN THE "BUILD BEFORE 21" MOVEMENT

Why Community Is Your Next Level

Building alone gets lonely, and progress can stall when you hit the inevitable doubts, dead-ends, or slow months. That's why the most resilient, successful builders surround themselves with a circle of action-takers—even if they're spread across cities or continents. Build Before 21 was always meant as more than a book: it's a launchpad for a new wave of young creators, hustlers, and lifelong learners.

Whether you want accountability, collaborators, or simply a daily dose of encouragement, the "Build Before 21" community is here to make sure you never build in isolation.

How to Join and Engage

1. **Community Group Links:**
    - WhatsApp Mastermind (for daily/weekly check-ins)
    - Discord Server (resources, feedback, digital coworking, Q&As)
    - LinkedIn Circle (updates, featured stories, alumni meet-ups)

(Find up-to-date links at the back of this book or by emailing official.tanweersidd@gmail.com for a personal invite)

1. Introduce Yourself
    - Name, what you're building or want to build, and your #1 goal for the next 90 days.

- Share your biggest "aha moment" or action step from any chapter.

1. **Weekly Challenge Threads**
   - Every Monday: Share your week's goal for public accountability.
   - Every Friday: Post one win (big or small), plus one lesson or failure—this helps the group grow stronger and more open together.

2. **Feedback and Collaboration Calls**
   - Monthly Zoom sessions with guest builders, mentors, and the author.
   - "Pitch practice rounds"—get honest, safe feedback on your latest launch, resume, or idea.

What You'll Find Inside

- **Peer Accountability:** Progress updates, 100-day sprint companions, and story-sharing.
- **Learning Circles:** Topic-based study and project groups (coding, marketing, design, public speaking).
- **Spotlight Features:** Get your project, win, or build story featured in monthly newsletters or on social.
- **Builder's Help Desk:** Real-time answers to challenges, job postings, gig swaps, and crowdsourced solutions from others just like you.

Signature Prompt: Your Community Commitment

"If you want to go fast, go alone. If you want to go far, go together."

- Post your "I'm a builder" intro in the group; tag a friend to join.
- Offer help at least once for every request you make—this keeps the community thriving.
- Set a calendar reminder: first Saturday each month = "Community Check-In."

Real Builder Story: Growth by Association

I've seen shy students become bold leaders, stuck projects turn into funded startups, and lifelong friendships form—all because someone took the risk to reach out and join a like-minded circle. When you show up for the group, the group shows up for you.

Takeaway: Never Build Alone Again

No matter your background, age, resource level, or starting line—there's a seat for you at this table.
Bring your mess, your spark, your ambition.

The next chapter of your journey is richer (and faster) when shared.
On the following pages: Learn more about the author's journey, discover how to stay connected, and find a running list of notes, references, and a space for your own reflections. Your story is now part of a movement—let's keep building, together.

ABOUT THE AUTHOR – TANWEER SIDD

Who Is Tanweer Sidd?

From small-town dreamer in Lucknow to award-winning entrepreneur, mentor, and movement builder, Tanweer's journey is proof that age, location, and resources are no match for relentless action, honesty, and community.

Starting with a battered laptop, Rs.500 in savings, and more doubts than roadmaps, Tanweer hustled his way through power cuts, rejection emails, and "you're too young" stares.

His startups—built out of modest hostel rooms and neighborhood cafes—have helped hundreds of students launch side hustles, discover digital skills, and break free from the "wait until you're older" trap.

Builder. Teacher. Story-Sharer.

Tanweer doesn't just create companies—he's obsessed with demystifying the startup journey for Gen Z, especially those coming from backgrounds with zero "network," privilege, or fancy degrees.

He speaks at universities, hosts live challenges, and actively replies to messages from young builders across India, offering practical advice, tough love, and a deep belief that "ordinary people, starting early, can create extraordinary futures."

What fuels his writing, workshops, and business philosophy?

- Breaking the myth that "success" requires luck or perfect timing
- Transforming personal failures into shareable, actionable blueprints
- Building generous communities where learning, failing, and winning happen together

Let's Connect and Grow Together

- **Email**: official.tanweersidd@gmail.com
- **LinkedIn/Instagram**: @tanweersidd (for daily micro-lessons, templates, and new project announcements)
- **Community:** Join the "Build Before 21" mastermind via WhatsApp, Discord, and live Q/A events (details earlier in this book)

Signature Prompt: Your Turn to Write

"Every builder is a teacher, and every student deserves a story they can see themselves in."

Take a moment:

- What's one story from your life, big or small, that could teach (or encourage) someone just one step behind you?
- Write it, share it, or send it to Tanweer—you might inspire the next builder in the movement.

Final Note

Thank you for letting my journey, my lessons, and my failures walk beside you through these pages. If you ever feel like giving up, remember: you're part of a new wave—a generation of builders who won't settle for "some day."

Keep building, keep sharing.
We're in this together.
— Tanweer Sidd

NOTES & REFERENCES

Why Notes Matter

No book can anticipate every question, insight, or "aha!" moment you'll have along your journey. The best builders don't just read—they engage, highlight, scribble side remarks, and link new lessons back to their own experience. This page is your dedicated space to capture all the ideas, sparks, and resources that inspired you as you read Build Before 21.

How to Use This Section

Personal Notes:

- Use these lines for anything that stood out—quotes you want to remember, lessons that hit hard, prompts to revisit, or action steps worth repeating.

References:

- Jot down the most useful books, articles, podcasts, mentors, or websites you discovered during your journey here.
- (See previous Resource and Template pages for favorites recommended by the author.)

Ideas in Motion:

- Any time you see a template or worksheet idea you want to adapt, note it here and update your own "Builder's Vault."

• **Your Notes**

Key References to Explore Further

- Atomic Habits by James Clear
- Show Your Work! by Austin Kleon
- The Lean Startup by Eric Ries
- YouTube: Traversy Media, Ali Abdaal, Abhi and Niyu
- Google Digital Garage, HubSpot Academy
- Podcasts: The Tim Ferriss Show, Masters of Scale

As you keep building, keep adding to these lines. Your own notes and references will eventually become your personalized blueprint, tailored from real action, lived lessons, and the communities you join. **Remember—every great builder is always a student, taking notes for the next breakthrough. This section belongs to your story now.**

[More blank pages are provided after this point to continue your notes and idea]

BLANK NOTES – FOR YOUR BUILDER'S IDEAS, SKETCHES & PLANS

Your Space to Ideate, Reflect, and Create

This page—and the ones that follow—belong only to you. Every great project, product, partnership, or pivot begins with raw, unfiltered ideas scrawled in the margins:

- Lightbulb moments
- Growth hacks you want to try
- "Next steps" brainstormed during lunch
- Lessons or feedback from your first customers
- Mini-maps for your next 100-day challenge
- Encouraging words from mentors, peers, or even your future self

Tips for Using Your Notes Pages

- Doodle, map, draw mindsets or systems.
- Sometimes a simple sketch says more than a page of text.
- Paste in clippings or printouts:
- Screenshots of wins, notes from community, favorite quotes, or inspirational stories.
- Create a Builder's Log:
- Make a running diary of wins, breakthroughs, and lessons. Mark each date—you'll be amazed at how far you've come over the months ahead.

Free-Write Weekly Reviews:

- Every Sunday, jot down:
    - What went well?
    - Where did you get stuck?
    - What will you test or try next week?

This Page is Your Launchpad

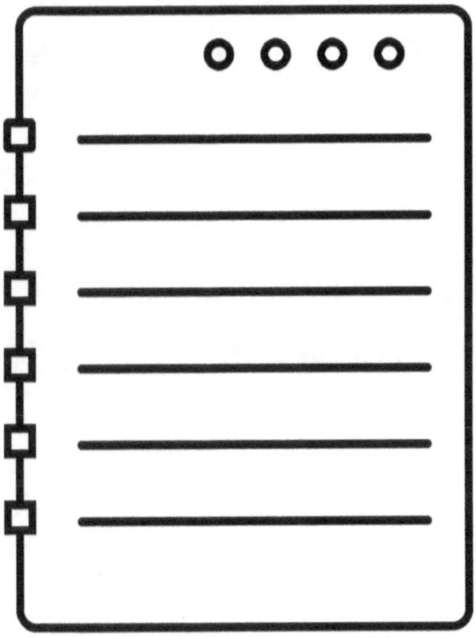

Keep filling these pages with what matters most to you.

Your ideas are the real seeds of every future build.

The building doesn't stop here—keep writing, dreaming, and acting.

Your next big story starts with a single line on this page.

BLANK NOTES – YOUR BUILDER'S WORKBOOK (CONTINUED)

Every Big Move Starts Here

This page is intentionally left blank for you to expand, reflect, and capture your building journey in real time. Use it as a canvas for brainstorming, journaling, or outlining your next project. Many of the world's bright ideas began in the unnoticed corners of notebooks—yours could be next.

Ideas, Tasks, Goals, and More

- Sketch your next product or startup idea.
- List questions for mentors or ideas to share in the "Build Before 21" community.
- Journal your learnings from every chapter, action sheet, or experiment.
- Map out a weekly sprint plan, create a mind map, or paste in concept clippings.

- ....
- ....
- ....
- ....
- ....
- ....
- ....
- ....

Signature Prompt:

"These pages belong to only one builder: you. Every empty line is a chance to change your story."

Use as many blank pages as you need—your builder's notebook is never truly finished.

Blank Notes – Your Builder's Workbook (Continued)

Use This Space for Breakthroughs

Use this page is yours for anything that keeps your momentum alive:

- Brainstorm new products, features, features, or startup concepts
- Record challenges and how you solved them
- List names of mentors, collaborators, supporters you meet along your journey
- Document your learning sprints, experiments, or feedback snapshots
- Plan your next 100-day builder sprint, including targets, tasks, and motivation hacks
- ....
- ....
- ....
- ....

Signature Prompt: Build It ON Paper First

"The world's boldest launches start as scribbles. Let these empty lines be the birthplace of your first (or next) big win."

Keep going. Every great builder's notebook is filled with crossed-out drafts, lightning-bolt ideas, and... the stubborn belief that the next breakthrough could be just one page away

.

Use as many blank pages as needed. Your story is still growing—write it, sketch it, and build it, page by page.

Blank Notes – Builder's Creative Sandbox

Expand. Sketch. Dream. Plan.

This page is another blank canvas for your ongoing builder's journey. It's designed for whatever you need most—messy brainstorming, project mind-maps, vision boards, or reminders of what you're building next. No prompt, no expectation—just pure space for your thoughts, ideas, and breakthroughs.

Possible Uses

- Bullet your next week's action steps.
- Draw diagrams, timelines, or workflows for current projects.
- Paste in motivational quotes, feedback, or screenshots of your wins.
- Draft outreach scripts or workshop lesson plans.
- Reflect on what the last 40 pages sparked and how you'll turn learning into momentum.
- ....
- ....
- ....
- ....

Signature Prompt: Let This Be Your Launchpad

"Every idea that changed a life started as a scribble in the margins. Fill these lines with possibility."

Use as many pages as you need—Builder's notebooks are never truly full. Your story keeps growing from here

SOCIAL MEDIA PRESENCE

@tanweer_sidd

AUTHOR'S WEBSITE

SiDD

siddinfotech.com

TANWEER SIDD

tanweersidd.com

www.ingramcontent.com/pod-product-compliance
Lightning Source LLC
Chambersburg PA
CBHW050020170726
48282CB00025B/473
9789334360332